SOARING EAGLE SCHOOL OF THE SPIRIT I

GABRIELE GILPIN

SOARING EAGLE SCHOOL OF THE SPIRIT I

Copyright © 2016
Gabriele Gilpin
All rights reserved.
ISBN: 0692672354
ISBN-13: 978-0692672358 (Soaring Eagle Ministries, Inc.)

Soaring Eagle Ministries, Inc.
10990 Ft. Caroline Road # 350352
Jacksonville, FL 32225
Visit us online: www.soaringeagleinc.org

No part of this book may be reproduced in any form or by any electronic or mechanical means without prior permission in writing from the publisher.

Printed in the United States of America.

Unless otherwise indicated, all Scriptures taken from the New King James Version. Other versions are abbreviated as follows:
AMP (Amplified Bible), (NIV) New International Version

TABLE OF CONTENTS

	INTRODUCTION	
1	FOUNDATIONS OF FAITH	1
2	MATURING – IT'S TIME TO GROW UP	17
3	MOTIVATIONAL GIFTS	29
4	GIFTS OF THE HOLY SPIRIT	39
5	FRUIT OF THE HOLY SPIRIT	51
6	THE FIVE FOLD MINISTRY	65
7	VISION CASTING	75
	ABOUT THE AUTHOR	82

INTRODUCTION

For over two decades, Gabriele Gilpin has traveled to towns, villages, cities, regions and nations around the globe to encourage, equip and empower leaders using biblical training, passionate preaching and activation through the gifts of the Holy Spirit with demonstration of the power of God's Spirit. The gifts of God are in need of being fanned to flame – and stirred up!

The glorious result of equipping and building up leaders in the Body of Christ is seen in the multiplication of more leaders. Following are some scriptures to meditate on:

2 Timothy 4:2 "Preach the Word!"

Matthew 24:14 "And His Gospel of the kingdom will be preached in all the world as a witness to all the nations, and then the end will come."

2 Timothy 4:5b "fulfill your ministry"

2 Timothy 2:2 "And the things that you have heard from me among many witnesses, commit these to faithful people who will be able to teach others also.."

Following are some pointers to focus on and to be aware of for your ongoing training.

The purpose of Ministry is: "for the equipping of the saints for the work of service, to the building up of the body of Christ" (Ephesians 4:12)

Equipping is more than just teaching and should always include impartation and activation. Think about this….. a soldier enlisted in the Armed Forces is taught about weapons and battle strategies in a classroom setting. Afterwards they are taken into the field and released and activated to implement what they have been taught.

- It is vital to only invest into the perfect will of God for you ~ Romans 12:2

- Put your efforts into things that produce Kingdom results, Kingdom manifestations, Kingdom harvest, and distance yourself from any other projects that causes you to be distracted from your true calling!

- Focus on and thrive in the place of your gifting and anointing

SOARING EAGLE SCHOOL OF THE SPIRIT I

1

FOUNDATIONS OF FAITH

Eye has not seen and ear has not heard and it has not entered into the heart of man, everything that God has prepared for those who love Him. But He has unveiled and revealed them by His Spirit. For the Holy Spirit searches deeply, examining all, even the profound and endless things of the Father.

For what person knows and understands what passes through a man's thoughts except the man's own spirit within him? Just so no one discerns or comes to know and comprehend the thoughts of God except the Spirit of God.

We have received the Holy Spirit that we might understand, appreciate and welcome the gifts of divine favor, grace and love so freely and lavishly bestowed on us by the Father.

And we are setting these truths forth in words not taught by human wisdom but taught by the Holy Spirit combining and interpreting spiritual truths with spiritual language to those who possess the Holy Spirit.

But the natural, non-spiritual man does not accept or welcome or admit into his heart the gifts and teachings and revelations of the Spirit of God, for they are folly and meaningless nonsense to him; and He is incapable of knowing them because they are spiritually discerned.
 (See 1 Corinthians 2:9-15 Amp paraphrased)

From this passage of scripture, we learn that God's truth can only be understood by the Spirit. The Lord reveals His truth to those who love Him and He has sent the Holy Spirit, who is the spirit of Truth, leading us into God's Truth. He will also reveal Jesus to us and He will show us what is to come. Therefore, ask the Holy Spirit to be your Teacher and ask Him to give you revelation and spiritual insight.

Dear Father of Glory, God of our Lord Jesus Christ,

I ask for the spirit of wisdom and revelation, of insight into mysteries and secrets, in the deep and intimate knowledge of Jesus.

Flood my heart with Your Light. Allow me to apprehend the wonderful future You have for me. Help me understand the incredible greatness of Your power towards me, the same resurrection power that raised Jesus from the dead and seated Him high above every principality and power, and put all things under His feet.

Lord fill me to overflowing with the fullness of Your Presence and Glory. I ask this in Jesus' name.
Ephesians 1:15-19

****

If you base your faith on a Firm Foundation ~ You will not be Shaken!

We are all in need of a Firm Foundation built upon the only true foundation, which is on Christ Jesus. As Apostle Paul, the wise master builder, taught us in the following scripture.

1 Corinthians 3:11
For no other foundation can anyone lay than that which is laid, which is Jesus Christ.

It is vital, as the Body of Christ, to mature individually and corporately. This study is starting out with laying the scriptural foundation and then building upon it. After laying a foundation on the one that has already been established, we will continue with equipping for ministry and business.

So let's start with the following foundational teachings - the truths that cannot be compromised. The Deity of the Lord Jesus Christ is found in the following Foundation Scriptures:

In the beginning was the Word, and the Word was with God, and the Word was God. John 1:1-2

Jesus said to them, "Most assuredly, I say to you, before Abraham was, I AM. John 8:58

I and the Father are One. John 10:30

His Virgin Birth

Isaiah 7:14 AMP – *Therefore the Lord Himself shall give you a sign; Behold, the young woman who is unmarried and a virgin shall conceive and bear a son, and shall call his name Immanuel (God with us).*
Luke 1:26-38

His Sinless Life

1 John 3:5 – *And you know that He was manifested to take away our sins, and in Him there is no sin.*

Hebrews 7:26-28 – *Jesus, our perfect High Priest*
1 Peter 2:22

His Miracles

Acts 2:22 AMP
Acts 10:38 – *How God anointed Jesus of Nazareth with the Holy Spirit and with power; who went about doing good, and healing all that were oppressed of the devil; for God was with Him.*
John 2:11
John 2:23
John 3:1-2
John 20:30-31

His Substitutionary Work at the Cross

2 Corinthians 5:21 – *For He made Him who knew no sin to be sin for us, that we might become the righteousness of God in Him.*
Hebrews 9:28a – *So Christ was offered once to bear the sins of many.*
1 Peter 2:24a
1 John 2:2
1 John 4:10
Colossians 1:22 AMP
Hebrews 2:17
Romans 4:24b-25
2 Timothy 2:11 AMP
Colossians 1:13-14
Revelation 1:5-6

His Bodily Resurrection from the Dead

Matthew 28:5-6
1 Corinthians 15:3-4 – *He was buried, and rose again on the third day*
Acts 2:23-28 – *God raised Jesus from the dead, because it was not possible for death to hold Him.*

His Exaltation to the Right Hand of God

Acts 1:9-11 – *This same Jesus, who was taken up from you into heaven, will so come in like manner as you saw Him go into heaven.*
Acts 2:32-36
Hebrews 1:1-3
Philippians 2:9-11

<u>Biblical Foundation</u>

The most important thing for a follower of Jesus Christ is to build a strong foundation. This is especially important in light of the ever-changing uncertainties of modern life. Therefore, we must have the kind of foundation that can withstand any spiritual opposition. *Jesus said, "Everyone who comes to Me, and hears My words, and acts upon them is like a man building a house, who dug deep and laid a foundation upon the rock" (Luke 6:47-48).* This is what we will endeavor to have - a firm foundation put in place, even so it will never be seen to the physical eye, but as Jesus pointed out, that the house stands even when the storms come. But He also added, the foolish man who hears His words and fails to act upon them is like the man who builds his house without foundation. The storm comes and wipes him out and reveals the faulty foundation.

Let's consider some of those foundational biblical teachings vital for our spiritual growth. Remember the early church turned their world upside down, without the internet, twitter or Facebook, airplanes, and huge sound systems. The world around them witnessed the reality of a risen Christ within them, and that the disciples had become new creations, who truly followed Him. They were armed and dangerous spiritually and withstood the pressure, threats and temptations. They were ready to lay down their lives for the cause of Jesus Christ. Let us become "Overcoming Fiery Believers" influencing regions with eyes to see and ears to hear, wide awake and soaring as eagles!

Salvation

A revelation about why people need a savior and what someone needs to be saved from is essential. When we turn to Jesus, repent from our sins, and accept Him as our Lord and Savior, we enter into the place of being "born again". We experience a new birth and are given a new heart. We become partakers of eternal life; eternal life is in the Son of God. Jesus said because I live, you shall also live. When we pass from this life we shall be instantly with the Lord.

-a changed life/a new creation

Sinful man's condition:
Romans 3:9-20, 23

What are the wages of sin?
Romans 6:23

God's solution for sin
John 3:16, 17

Receiving Jesus as Lord and Savior
John 1:12-13
Romans 10:9-10
1 Peter 1:23
1 John 4:7
Acts 2:37
2 Corinthians 5:17
Therefore, if anyone is in Christ, he is a new creation; old things have passed away; behold, all things have become new.

Temple of the Holy Spirit

1 Corinthians 6:19-20
Or do you not know that your body is the temple of the Holy Spirit who is in you, whom you have from God, and you are not your own? [20] *For you were bought at a price; therefore glorify God in your body and in your spirit, which are God's.*

Water Baptism

In Water Baptism we bury our old nature and rise to walk with Christ in newness of life. Water baptism is a supernatural experience that is imperative for experiencing new life in God's kingdom. It is a step of obedience and proclamation of the newness of life we are walking in.

Romans 6:1-4
What shall we say then? Shall we continue in sin that grace may abound? 2 Certainly not! How shall we who died to sin live any longer in it? 3 Or do you not know that as many of us as were baptized into Christ Jesus were baptized into His death? 4 Therefore we were buried with Him through baptism into death, that just as Christ was raised from the dead by the glory of the Father, even so we also should walk in newness of life.

Acts 2:38-39
Then Peter said to them, "Repent, and let every one of you be baptized in the name of Jesus Christ for the remission of sins; and you shall receive the gift of the Holy Spirit. 39 For the promise is to you and to your children, and to all who are afar off, as many as the Lord our God will call."

Colossians 2:11-13

Living under Open Heaven

Matthew 3:16-17
When Jesus was water baptized in the Jordan River by John the Baptist, the heavens were opened and he saw the Spirit of God descending like a dove, and lighting upon him and a voice from heaven, saying, this is my beloved Son, in whom I am well pleased.

Baptism of the Holy Spirit and Fire

Matthew 3:11
Acts 1:8

But you shall receive power when the Holy Spirit has come upon you; and you shall be witnesses to Me in Jerusalem, and in all Judea and Samaria, and to the end of the earth."

Acts 4:31-33
31 And when they had prayed, the place where they were assembled together was shaken; and they were all filled with the Holy Spirit, and they spoke the word of God with boldness. 32 Now the multitude of those who believed were of one heart and one soul; neither did anyone say that any of the things he possessed was his own, but they had all things in common. 33 And with great power the apostles gave witness to the resurrection of the Lord Jesus. And great grace was upon them all,"

Word of God and Spiritual Hunger

Acts 19:20 – *So the word of the Lord grew mightily and prevailed.*
Acts 12:24 – *But the word of God grew and multiplied.*
Job 23:12
Psalm 84:1, 2, 10

The Power of God is in and on the Word

Romans 1:16 – *For I am not ashamed of the gospel of Christ, for it is the power of God to salvation for everyone who believes, for the Jew first and also for the Greek.*

The Word of God is truth and effectively works within you who believe

1 Thessalonians 2:13

The Word of Faith and Hope

Hebrews 11:1 – *Now faith is the substance of things hoped for, the evidence of things not seen.*

Abraham's faith in God's Word to him brought God's promise to pass.

The Power of the Word on our Lips

Acts 6:7 – *Then the word of God spread, and the number of the disciples multiplied greatly in Jerusalem, and a great many of the priests were obedient to the faith.*

2 Timothy 4:2 – *Preach the word! Be ready in season and out of season. Convince, rebuke, exhort, with all longsuffering and teaching.*

The Word causes us to Love

John 13:34-35
1 John 4:7-8
1 John 3:14
1 John 2:10 AMP

The Word is Living and Powerful

Ephesians 6:17
And take the helmet of salvation, and the sword of the Spirit, which is the word of God;

Hebrews 4:12
For the word of God is living and powerful, and sharper than any two-edged sword, piercing even to the division of soul and spirit, and of joints and marrow, and is a discerner of the thoughts and intents of the heart.

The Blood

Foundation Scriptures: Matthew 26:28-29

The Blood of Jesus Redeems us from Sin

1 Peter 1:18-19 AMP
Ephesians 1:7
Acts 20:28

The Blood of Jesus Reconciles us to the Father

Isaiah 6:4-7
Romans 3:23 – *For all have sinned and fall short of the glory of God*
Colossians 1:19-22
Ephesians 2:13 – *But now in Christ Jesus you who once were far off have been brought near by the blood of Christ.*

The Blood of Jesus allows us to come boldly before the Father

Hebrews 10:19-23
Hebrews 4:15-16

The Blood of Jesus and the Word of Testimony gives us the power to overcome

Revelation 12:11 – *And they overcame him by the blood of the Lamb and by the word of their testimony, and they did not love their lives to the death.*
1 Corinthians 15:57

The Blood of Jesus is held in honor in heaven

We reign as kings and priests on the earth through the blood of Jesus.

Revelations 5:9-10 – *And they sang a new song, saying: "You are worthy to take the scroll, And to open its seals; For You were slain, And have redeemed us to God by Your blood out ......And have made us kings and priests to our God; And we shall reign on the earth.*

Intimacy with the Father

James 4:8
Draw nigh to God, and he will draw nigh to you.

Jeremiah 31:3
The LORD hath appeared of old unto me, [saying], Yea, I have loved thee with an everlasting love: therefore with lovingkindness have I drawn you.

Ephesians 5:1
Be ye therefore followers of God, as dear children;

1 John 3:1
Behold what manner of love the Father has bestowed on us, that we should be called children of God! Therefore the world does not know us, because it did not know Him.

Prayer/Intercession

Vibrant and passionate
Romans 8:26-27
Likewise the Spirit also helps in our weaknesses. For we do not know what we should pray for as we ought, but the Spirit Himself

makes intercession for us with groanings which cannot be uttered. [27] *Now He who searches the hearts knows what the mind of the Spirit is, because He makes intercession for the saints according to the will of God.*

Worship in Spirit and Truth

John 4:23-24
But the hour is coming, and now is, when the true worshipers will worship the Father in spirit and truth; for the Father is seeking such to worship Him. [24] *God is Spirit, and those who worship Him must worship in spirit and truth."*

Mission/Great Commissioning

Matthew 28:18-20
[18] *And Jesus came and spoke to them, saying, "All authority has been given to Me in heaven and on earth.* [19] *Go therefore and make disciples of all the nations, baptizing them in the name of the Father and of the Son and of the Holy Spirit,* [20] *teaching them to observe all things that I have commanded you; and lo, I am with you always, even to the end of the age." Amen.*

Anointing of the Believers

Luke 4:18-19
"The Spirit of the Lord is upon Me, because He has anointed Me To preach the gospel to the poor; He has sent Me to heal the brokenhearted, To proclaim liberty to the captives And recovery of sight to the blind, To set at liberty those who are oppressed; [19] *To proclaim the acceptable year of the Lord."*

> *Hebrews 4:12*
> *For the word of God is living and powerful, and sharper than any two-edged sword, piercing even to the division of soul and spirit, and of joints and marrow, and is a discerner of the thoughts and intents of the heart.*

2

MATURING
IT'S TIME TO GROW UP

Every one of us began our walk with the Lord as spiritual babies in Christ. However, the Lord does not intend for us to stay that way. As Christians we have been given the abundant life of Jesus Christ and we can choose to grow from immaturity to become mature sons of God.

We are living in a time of transitioning and things are changing and shifting seemingly all the time. The winds of change are blowing and many new connections have been made in order to fitly join the body of Christ. We can sense, that these are new times graced with open doors of opportunity and rapid fulfilment of prayers that have been lingering for some time.

These developments and the spiritual growth into maturity as sons and daughters will cause us to be a formidable force in times of utter chaos. Empowering us to do all we can in the power of His might and then STAND in and on the promises of our Father.

Soaring higher and yet impacting by going deeper, as we witness Heaven invading earth, and Kingdom manifestations of God's glory to erupt throughout His beloved world.

John 3:16
For God so loved the world that He gave His only begotten Son, that whoever believes in Him should not perish but have everlasting life.

As I travel the nations, I see that the Lord is elevating His people to the next level in ministry or professions and personal lives. We are moved forward in our destinies, advancing us in His purpose and training us for greater influence. Through all of this, His kingdom can be established in every sphere of society.

When the Lord begins to shift you from one assignment to the next, you will need to go through a season of preparation. This preparation requires more humility and a child-like faith to be teachable in order to receive a transformation from the inside out. Moving forward to your new level will require discipline and a deep love for your heavenly Father, seeking Him and receiving His wisdom.

Let me encourage you with some words of wisdom from the book of Daniel. Concerning the times and seasons of our lives, Daniel 2:21 teaches us that *"He [God] changes times and seasons; he sets up kings and deposes them. He gives wisdom to the wise and knowledge to the discerning"* (NIV).

YIELDING

It is a time of submitting and praying for spiritual growth. If we yield to our born again spirit, we can see that our spirit man has five senses just as we have our natural five senses. We are asking for our eyes to be opened to see in the realm of heaven – we can see the throne of God, we can see the glory of God and with hearing ears we can hear what the Spirit is saying to the church. We can hear things other people can't hear. We can even hear the angels singing and just as Apostle John, when he heard the voice like a trumpet calling him to come up higher, through the open door, to hear what the Lord wanted to show him. (Revelations 4).

Let's grow up and mature, since we read in Romans 8, that even creation is groaning for the revealing of the true sons of God....those who are mature, walking in the Spirit.

WHO ARE WE IN CHRIST?

SCRIPTURE: Colossians 3:1-17
Colossians 3:1 "If then you were raised with Christ, seek those

things which are above, where Christ is, sitting at the right hand of God. 2 Set your mind on things above, not on things on the earth. 3 For you died, and your life is hidden with Christ in God."

In response to my desire to learn how to grow into maturity, I wrote the following accounts years ago. This may inspire you to locate your current stage of spiritual growth and a desire to abide and to walk in a closer, more intimate fellowship with the Father, Son and the Holy Spirit.

It requires renewing your mind by washing by the water of the Word of God daily. Giving our body as a living sacrifice, holy and acceptable unto God (see Romans 12:1-2). Additionally, by exercising your senses to discern the difference between the natural man, carnal man and the spiritual man.

****

INFANT

"As newborn babes, desire the sincere milk of the word, that you may grow thereby." 1 Peter 2:2

When I was first born again by the Spirit of God and the water, I remember experiencing the love of God in such a pure form. It was God's unconditional love and I knew without a shadow of a doubt, Jesus would have died just for me, even if I was the only one on earth.

My hunger and thirst for the things of God seemed to be insatiable. Since I wanted to know much more about Him, I was constantly in the Word of God. My entire world changed; even the flowers seemed brighter, the grass was greener and I felt lighter, almost like I was floating on air.

During this time my spiritual mom would spend time with me and I was able to share what was on my heart. She never looked down at me, nor was shocked by what I was saying. She would listen and then suggested we should go to Jesus in prayer with all of these issues. Therefore, I learned to run to Jesus in every situation. Jesus would give me scriptures and they would always speak to me and bring understanding and direction.

My deepest desire was to share Jesus with everything that moved. The Lord delivered me from addictions and bad habits. Because I was a new creation in Christ, I did not have the desire to do what I used to do anymore.

My babyhood was a sweet and precious time, learning about the Lord and the Holy Spirit. I never forget the mercy, compassion and loving kindness I received from the Father.

This kind of love brought me through the growing pains of infancy. But I was still easily offended, hurt, distracted and depressed. I had attacks of depression, which caused me to want to run and hide. My walk with the Lord strengthened me and healed me and soon I was able to help others at times.

The above scripture in 1 Peter 2:2 speaks to me, because I can see how I desired the sincere milk of the Word, by listening to the Word and spending much time with Jesus. The word of God and circumstances I was facing were used by the Holy Spirit to cause me to grow up.

When we are first grafted into the vine, the Lord gives us many props to stabilize us and to help us to deepen our walk and growth. But after I was getting used to all of these props and started to be strengthened, the Lord knew exactly when to remove one prop after another. I felt these props holding me up, but as I grew, my ability to draw from Jesus, and to be that branch (see John 15:5), became increasingly more evident. It is not the branch that bears the fruit, but the branch abides in the Lord and allows the fruit to grow.

Eventually my spiritual mom, who was one of my props, moved away and thereafter I moved to another place and had to rely on Jesus completely. Hence all my props were removed. This caused me to grow up in a more rapid pace. Not to mention I was under some very wonderful teaching, which required me to shift accordingly and I remember going to Jesus to hear from Him on a consistent basis. Sometimes the milk a baby receives can be sour, which could be a false teaching or wolves in sheep's clothing attacking. The gift of discernment would always point out when the milk was sour and I turned from it.

It was time to grow up and as David said: *"Surely I have behaved and quieted myself, as a child that is weaned of his mother; my soul is even as a weaned child." Psalm 131:2.* The Bible says concerning Isaac, *"And the child grew, and was weaned; and Abraham made a great feast the same day that Isaac was weaned." (Genesis 21:8).*

What an amazing day, when Christians grow enough to get off the baby bottle and are embarking on the next stage of childhood.

****

CHILD

As Jesus was always available for me and as I trusted Him more and more, I knew He would never leave me nor forsake me (see Hebrews 13:5) and I stepped into the childhood phase.

"That we henceforth be no more children... Ephesians 4:14

It was time to grow up and mature concerning the things of God. During that time I was placed in a team of believers and we did outreaches and had to work with one another. Spending extensive time with other Christians caused all sorts of hidden things to come to the surface. At this point, I was still very unsure, insecure and full of worry and anxiety. But the Lord taught me through His Word:

"Casting all your care upon Him for He cares for you." 1 Peter 5:7

Part of my insecurity and anxiety was taken when I realized that the Father, Son and the Holy Spirit care about me and I can trust God to handle all situations in my life. I can lean on Him, because He has my best interest in His loving, caring heart. The reason why I battled rejection and abandonment issues was because of my past negative experiences and I was trying to be perfect. Instead of helping, it only caused me to be more anxious and I was not able to trust anyone.

Other people have sinned against me, but Jesus Christ is the same yesterday, today and forever. He never changes and He is always the same. Therefore, I can completely rely upon Him.

We grow up spiritually when we are able to forgive others and release them into the Father's hands and treat them with the same care and love the Father has shown us.

Matthew 6:34
Therefore do not worry about tomorrow, for tomorrow will worry about its own things. Sufficient for the day is its own trouble.

How wonderful, I do not have to worry about tomorrow anymore. I can fully enjoy today. As a matter of fact, I can enjoy this very moment without fretting and trying to figure out what I need to do, which is such a relief!

Freely I can come to Jesus like a child and He will tell me what He requires. Another way to grow up is by allowing God's hand to move in every circumstance. My prayer is: "Lord, not my will, but Your will be done. Lord, here I am send me."

1 John 4:18
There is no fear in love; but perfect love casts out fear, because fear involves torment. But he who fears has not been made perfect in love.

One day the Lord revealed to me that I had tremendous fear and shame in me. Shame is a "thief of intimacy". When I am ashamed it robs me of the intimacy with the Trinity and also with other loved ones. Jesus' perfect love delivered me from shame and He has given me double for my trouble!

During a mission trip, the Lord showed me that I was absolutely fine with Jesus, and I had fun with the Holy Spirit, but when it came to my Heavenly Father I had the urge to run away. Why? The abuse I received as a child painted the wrong picture in my mind. The stronghold of this wrong thinking was finally destroyed by His anointing.

After I was delivered of this torment, because fear and shame comes with and involves torment, I was able to receive the Father's love freely and give it away freely!

It is very clear to me that I am loved of my Father. As long as I walk in love, then I walk in the Father's realm, for God is love! His very nature, because He is love, compels Him to care for us, protect us, and shield us.

The Lord is my Shepherd. He feeds, guides and shields me! I shall not want…there is no lack. I have everything I need!

****

ADULT

Luke 6:45
A good man out of the good treasure of his heart brings forth good; and an evil man out of the evil treasure of his heart brings forth evil. For out of the abundance of the heart his mouth speaks.

In order to walk as an adult, my heart needed a major Holy Spirit check-up. We have "gates" representing the mind, eyes and ears. Whatever I receive into these gates and do not take authority over it, leaving it unchecked, eventually will travel into my heart, take root there and eventually will come out of my mouth giving life to certain fruit. After receiving this revelation, I was praying for the Holy Spirit's help and as I continued in His Word on a daily basis, my mind was renewed. The root causes were pulled out of my heart and, in turn, what came out of my mouth changed drastically. Now I was sowing righteous seeds bringing a harvest of eternal promises.

3 John 2
Beloved, I pray that you may prosper in all things and be in health, just as your soul prospers.

God desires to prosper us with spiritual, physical, emotional and material prosperity. The prosperity provided is part of being completely made whole; spirit, soul and body. When my soul is "sick", I will always experience lack in one way or another. But Jesus has called me to be whole, delivered from torment and bondage, healed from all sickness and disease. He has become poor, so I can be rich. Rich in love and life overflowing in abundance through Christ Jesus.

1 Corinthians 1:30
But of Him you are in Christ Jesus, who became for us wisdom from God—and righteousness and sanctification and redemption...

2 Corinthians 8:9
For you know the grace of our Lord Jesus Christ, that though He was rich, yet for your sakes He became poor, that you through His poverty might become rich.

The Holy Spirit comes and starts releasing healing and deliverance. After all, we have been taken out of darkness and translated into His marvelous light. The complete walk of wholeness in every area of my life can be maintained when I am whole in Jesus.

It is the Lord Who drives out the enemy before us. When the Holy Spirit is dealing with certain situations, there will be an ability to keep the freedom we have obtained! **Whom the Son sets free is free indeed!**

1 Corinthians 3:1
And I, brethren, could not speak to you as to spiritual people but as to carnal, as to babes in Christ.

The Corinthian church was known for using the gifts of the Holy Spirit, yet they still were very carnal (fleshly). There is obviously truth to the fact, that we need both the gifts and the fruit of the Holy Spirit to be in operation. To grow up into maturity, the fruit of the Holy Spirit (see Galatians 5:22, 23) has to develop and ripen.

After all, faith works by and through love and as long as we abide in Him, He will abide in us. Jesus desires for me to walk in step with Him, listening to Him, receiving from Him, the fountain of Living Water. I am delighted that Jesus will finish the good work He started within me. My deep desire is for His will and I continue to seek His perfect timing for everything that concerns my life.

3

MOTIVATIONAL GIFTS

ROMANS 12:4-8

For as we have many members in one body, but all the members do not have the same function, 5 so we, being many, are one body in Christ, and individually members of one another. 6 Having then gifts differing according to the grace that is given to us, let us use them: if prophecy, let us prophesy in proportion to our faith; 7 or ministry, let us use it in our ministering; he who teaches, in teaching; 8 he who exhorts, in exhortation; he who gives, with liberality; he who leads, with diligence; he who shows mercy, with cheerfulness.

As one body of Christ, God has given each believer one or more of these gifts outlined in Romans 12:4-8. Many believers exhibit more than one gift, but almost always, one is dominant. Each gift affects the way that a person views all ministries.

Have you ever wondered: Why do I think and act the way I do?

How we hear and respond depends much on our Motivational gifts – The Lord speaks to us through those gifts, and we may not recognize it, because it seems natural to us. In this study, we discover how gifts affect our relationships and how using our gifts will bring joy.

Because we all mainly view ministry through our gifting, we need to take time to understand each other's motivational gifting and our personality.

When coming together as a team, it is very important to know yourself and to know the team. There are natural styles of personality and there are adaptive styles of personalities.

Let's look into this a bit further…

Characteristic of Prophecy Motivated People:

Prophecy/Perceiver: The eye of the body

- one who clearly perceives the will of God
- sees everything black or white
- identifies good and evil and hates evil
- easily perceives the character of individuals and groups
- encourages repentance that produces good fruit

- knows that acceptance of difficulties will produce positive personal brokenness
- views the Bible as the basis of truth and authority
- boldly operates on spiritual principles
- is eager to see own blind spots and to help others to see theirs
- called to intercession, prayer, prophetic acts to affect change
- wants to see God's will done
- strongly promotes the spiritual growth of others
- desires to be obedient to God at all cost
- has strong opinions and convictions
- visionaries: seeing things others don't and bring it to reality
- speak to situation and see change

Problem areas:

- tends to be judgmental and blunt
- is pushy trying to have others mature spiritually
- is intolerant of opinions and views that differ from own
- struggles with self-image problems

Characteristics of the Serving Motivated People:

Server: The hand of the body

One who loves to serve others. Another appropriate word is "doer".

- easily recognizes practical needs and is quick to meet them
- especially enjoys manual projects, jobs, and functions
- keeps everything in meticulous order, is a detail person with a good memory
- enjoys showing hospitality, will stay with something until it is completed
- has a hard time saying no to requests for help
- enjoys working on immediate goals vs. long-range goals
- shows love for others in deeds and actions more than words
- needs to feel appreciated
- feels greatest joy in doing something that is helpful
- does not want to lead others and projects
- prefers doing a job to delegating it, has a high energy level
- supports others who are in leadership
- views serving to be of primary importance in life
- sees the best in others, meet their needs and love people
- tending to the physical needs

Problem areas:

- can be critical of others who do not help out with obvious needs (Martha, Luke 10:38-42)
- may neglect own family's needs by being too busy helping others
- they can easily get overextended and neglect loving Jesus
- may become pushy or interfering in eagerness to help
- finds it hard to accept being served by others
- can be easily hurt when unappreciated

Characteristics of the Teaching Motivated People:

Teacher: The mind of the body

- one who loves to research and communicate truth and presents truth in a logical, systematic way
- loves to study; enjoys word studies
- prefers to use biblical illustrations rather than life illustrations
- can get upset when scripture is used out of context;
- feels concerned that truth be established in every situation
- emphasizes facts and the accuracy of words;
- checks out the source of knowledge of others who teach
- feels Bible study is foundational to the operation of all the gifts

- is self-disciplined
- is emotionally self-controlled
- has only a select circle of friends (rather enjoys a good book)

Problem areas:

- tends to neglect the practical application of truth
- is slow to accept viewpoints of others
- tends to develop pride in intellectual ability
- 1 Cor. 8:1 knowledge puffs up, but love builds up
- tends to be legalistic and dogmatic
- is easily sidetracked by new interests

Characteristic of the Exhortation Motivated People:

Exhorter: The mouth of the body

- one who loves to encourage others to live a victorious life
- extremely positive people, who can also be called encouragers
- focus on working with people
- loves to do personal counseling
- views trials as opportunities to grow personally
- accepts people as they are without judging
- focuses on working with people
- finds truth in experience and then validate in scripture

- encourages others to develop in their personal ministries
- will discontinue personal counseling if no effort to change is seen
- fluent in communication
- makes decisions easily
- always completes what started
- expects a lot of self and others
- needs a "sounding board" for bouncing off ideas and thoughts
- receives rapid fire impressions

Problem areas:

- tends to interrupt others
- outspokenly opinionated
- can become overly self-confident
- will use scriptures out of context in order to make a point
- high sensitivity to emotions

Characteristics of the Giving Motivated People:

Giver: The arms of the body

- one who loves to give freely of talent, time, possessions, energy and means to benefit others and advance the Gospel
- it could also be called "contributor"
- gives by the leading of the Holy Spirit

- believes God is the Source of his supply
- likes to get the best value for money spent
- possesses both natural and God-given wisdom
- quickly volunteers
- has strong belief in giving
- focuses on sharing the Gospel

Problem areas:

- may try to control how contributions are used
- tends to pressure others to give
- may use financial giving to get out of other responsibilities

Characteristics of Organizational Motivated People:

Administrator: The shoulders of the body

- one who loves to organize, lead, or direct
- facilitator and leader
- is highly motivated to organize that for which he's responsible
- expresses ideas and organization in ways that communicate clearly
- enjoys working on long-range goals and projects
- easily facilitates resources and people to accomplish task or goals
- wants to see things completed as quickly as possible

Problem areas:

- becomes upset when others do not share the same vision or goals
- can regress into "using" people to accomplish own goals
- so goal oriented that they can forget people should not be pushed to extremes
- tends to drive self and neglect personal and family needs
- can get overextended, take on too much

Characteristics of the Mercy Motivated People:

Mercy person: The heart of the body

- one who shows compassion, love and care
- is attracted to people who are hurting or in distress
- is more concerned for mental and emotional distress than physical
- is motivated to help people have right relationships with one another
- is trusting and trustworthy
- avoids conflicts and confrontations
- is typically cheerful and joyful
- loves to worship the Lord
- doesn't like to be rushed in a job or activity
- is ruled by the heart rather than the head
- rejoices to see others blessed and grieves when others hurt

- is a crusader for good causes
- intercedes for the hurts and problems of others

Problem areas:

- tends to be indecisive
- is often prone to take up another person's offense
- is easily hurt by others
- empathizes too much with the suffering of others
- affectionate nature is often misinterpreted

****

In closing allow me to point out, that according to Romans 12:1-5, all believers are to present themselves to God as a living sacrifice. Only through this dedication, can our motivational gifts be fully used for God's glory.

Furthermore, our minds need to be renewed, so we can know and discern God's will. Then we must have a right attitude about ourselves and others. Realizing we have been given faith to discern the gifts in the Body of Christ and work together as One in HIM.

4

GIFTS OF THE HOLY SPIRIT

1 Corinthians 12:4-11

There are diversities of gifts, but the same Spirit. [5] There are differences of ministries, but the same Lord. [6] And there are diversities of activities, but it is the same God who works all in all. [7] But the manifestation of the Spirit is given to each one for the profit of all: [8] for to one is given the word of wisdom through the Spirit, to another the word of knowledge through the same Spirit, [9] to another faith by the same Spirit, to another gifts of healings by the same Spirit, [10] to another the working of miracles, to another prophecy, to another discerning of spirits, to another different kinds of tongues, to another the interpretation of tongues. [11] But one and the same Spirit works all these things, distributing to each one individually as He wills.

There are precious and marvelous gifts of the Holy Spirit that are available and should be a well-known part of the manifestations and operation of the Body of Christ until Jesus Christ returns.

By discovering and being knowledgeable on how to receive and sharpen the gifts of the Holy Spirit, everyone in the Body of Christ can be operating and releasing the gifts to display God's signs, wonders and glory to impact the world.

1 Corinthians 12:1
Now concerning spiritual gifts, brethren, I do not want you to be ignorant.

The Apostle Paul exhorted the Body of Christ not to be ignorant concerning the gifts of the Holy Spirit provided for us. The word ignorant means "to be without knowledge, not to understand, unknown, to mistake"...just to name a few. Let's look into it a bit further to gain insight and understanding.

There are differences of gifts and there are nine gifts of the Holy Spirit. They are: the word of wisdom, the word of knowledge, gift of faith, gifts of healings, working of miracles, prophecy, discerning of spirits, different kinds of tongues and interpretation of tongues.

They are broken down into three categories:

Gifts of Revelation – Reveal Something
Words of Wisdom, Word of Knowledge, Discerning of Spirits

Gifts of Power – Do Something
Gift of Faith, Gifts of Healings, Working of Miracles

Gifts of Communication – Say Something
Gift of Prophecy, Different Kinds of Tongues, Interpretation of Tongues

****

Gifts of Revelation

Word of Wisdom

1 Corinthians 12:8a:
For to one is given the word of wisdom through the Spirit

This gift does not manifest through and by the human mind, rather it is wisdom from God and illuminates the mind to receive and understand the wisdom from above. It comes as a divine revelation from God and tells or shows what is going to take place in the future. It does not come by natural age, but it comes through relationship with the Father and requires for us to yield to the Holy Spirit. When the will of God is unknown, that is where the word of wisdom comes into play. The Lord will reveal the perfect will of God by His Spirit.

1 Corinthians 2:6-10

Word of Knowledge

1 Corinthians 12:8b
To another the word of knowledge through the same Spirit

This gift manifests a knowing of knowledge which exists pertaining to the past or in the present. It is a knowledge, which has not been seen by the receiver's eyes nor has it been heard before. It is a divine revelation that tells or shows us what is happening in the realm of the Spirit presently.

Example:

In Haiti during the ministry time, I had a Word of Knowledge. I knew that the Lord wanted to heal feet. As this Word of Knowledge was called out, almost everyone in the place stood up. When I started to pray for healing of the feet, I knew it was not only physical healing in the feet, but the Lord was also lining them up in their walk with Him. A straight and narrow path in agreement with the Father's will and purposes.

Discerning of Spirits

1 Corinthians 12:10a
To another the working of miracles, to another prophecy, to another discerning of spirits

The gift of discerning is a divine ability to see or discern in three areas:
- When the Holy Spirit is moving
- Discerning the presence of angels or demons
- False doctrines, false prophets, see the heart of a man as revealed by the Holy Spirit

Apostle Paul dealt with this issue when the woman, who had a spirit of divination kept: *"Following after Paul and us, she kept crying out, saying, "These men are bond-servants of the Most High God, who are proclaiming to you the way of salvation." 18 She continued doing this for many days. But Paul was greatly annoyed, and turned and said to the spirit, "I command you in the name of Jesus Christ to come out of her!" And it came out at that very moment." Luke 16:17-18*

Paul discerned correctly and moved by the love of God casting out the spirit from the woman.

The true gifts of the Spirit will never come forth out of criticism or a judgmental or hardened heart. It is vital to enter into God's rest and follow the peace of God, which is our umpire.

****

Gifts of Power

Gift of Faith

1 Corinthians 12:9a
To another faith by the same Spirit

The gift of faith is a power gift – gifts that do something.

It is a gift of divine supernatural manifestation from God to receive a miracle at a specific time, at a specific place, for a specific purpose. It is a supernatural ability to believe for miraculous results in the midst of impossible situations by believing in a supernatural God.

The gift of faith is His faith released to us and we can become like David facing Goliath. David looked at the circumstances with overcoming faith. It is the power of God operating, therefore the Holy Spirit is doing the supernatural. It does not make any sense to the natural, carnal mind.

Gifts of Healing

1 Corinthians 12:9b
To another gifts of healings by the same Spirit

The gift of healing is a supernatural intervention of God's healing power over sickness and disease without the help of natural means.

Here are some examples:

Healing of the Soul: *He heals the broken hearted and binds up their wounds. Luke 4:18*

Healing of the Body: *Then Jesus went about all the cities and villages, teaching in their synagogues, preaching the gospel of the kingdom, and healing every sickness and every disease among the people. Matthew 9:35*

Working of Miracles

1 Corinthians 12:10a
To another the working of miracles

The working of miracles is a supernatural gift to perform a miracle or an intervention of God in the course of nature. The gift of faith and miracles often flow together. If someone is raised from the dead, then very often the person has to be healed, as well as raised.

Signs, wonders and miracles are there to show-case the power of God. Many creative miracles happening, like a brand new ear drum forming, where there was none and amputated limbs growing.

****

Gifts of Communication

Gift of Prophecy

1 Corinthians 12:10
To another prophecy

The gift of prophecy can be defined as God-inspired utterance in a known language. This gift can manifest by edifying, encouraging, building up, strengthening and comfort.

"But he who prophesies speaks edification and exhortation and comfort to men." 1 Corinthians 14:3

Apostle Paul exhorted:
1 Corinthians 14:1
"Pursue love, and desire spiritual gifts, but especially that you prophecy."
1 Corinthians 14:39
"Therefore, brethren, desire earnestly to prophesy" Prophecy can be a forth telling of what the Holy Spirit is saying. Sometimes, we receive a prophetic direction in dreams or visions.

Different Kind of Tongues

1 Corinthians 12:10
To another different kinds of tongues

Diversities of Tongues (different kind of tongues) are regarded as a ministry. What the Word of God is talking about here in 1 Corinthians 12:28, 30 is ministering through tongues and interpretation to bless and help others in the assembly of the saints. Moving in different kind of tongues is available for ministering to others. Again it is not as I will, but as the Holy Spirit wills and directs.

It is the supernatural ability to speak in another language. A language that is completely unfamiliar to the one who speaks and is by the Holy Spirit. A wonderful example of this is found in the outpouring of the Holy Spirit on the day of Pentecost.

Acts 2:1-12
Every one of the 120 disciples, who were filled by the Holy Spirit in the upper room, came out and spoke in other languages. Others around were able to understand what the disciples were saying when speaking in tongues in their own language.

When I went to Kenya, Africa in the 1990's, I was speaking in tongues and the interpreter asked: "Did you know that you just spoke the salvation message in the language of Swahili?" It is possible to speak in another language and don't understand it, but others around will.

Another example: At a church service in Frankfurt, Germany, someone was speaking out loud in tongues. A couple from France sat in the back of the place, but after hearing the message in tongues, they stood up and testified, that this word was directly for them, because it was in French and it dealt with a situation they were facing! The gift of different tongues was in operation to bless this couple and the tongue was actually in another language, which was understood by them.

In these cases the gift of interpretation was not necessary, because an earthly language was spoken and there was someone who knew the language.

When someone speaks in tongues it can be the following reasons:

> ➤ Someone may speak to the Lord communicating the secrets of his heart (1 Cor. 14:2)
> ➤ For edifying himself (1 Cor. 14:4)
> ➤ Speaking in tongues to praise, glorify and exalt the Lord (Acts 2:11; 10:46)
> ➤ Intercession by the Holy Spirit (Romans 8:26)
> ➤ Giving a message of exhortation, edification, comfort and possibly a correction (1 Cor. 14:4, 22-25)
> ➤ An authoritative tongue spoken by God and it is Spirit to spirit (Isaiah 28:11)

Interpretation of Tongues

1 Corinthians 12:10
To another the interpretation of tongues

The teaching about the gifts of the Holy Spirit concludes with the last gift: the interpretation of tongues.

This gift always requires to come in a package of two, because the gift of speaking in different kind of tongues is necessary before it can be interpreted. Which means those two gifts are put together and they work in unison.

As mentioned before, there are times when this gift is not necessary, because a known language is spoken. The interpretation of tongues will discern which of the above tongues is in operation.

A Word of Caution

When we watch someone flow in the gifts of the Holy Spirit, it is not necessarily a sign of maturity. When someone operates in the fruit of the Holy Spirit it is a sign of maturity. The nine gifts of the Holy Spirit do not belong to us, in the sense of us operating in them as we want. Instead it is always AS THE SPIRIT WILLS. It is a choice to walk in the fruit, but to walk in the gifts is a privilege.

Galatians 5:22-25

But the fruit of the Spirit is love, joy, peace, patience, kindness, goodness, faithfulness, [23] gentleness, self-control. Against such there is no law. [24] And those who are Christ's have crucified the flesh with its passions and desires. [25] If we live in the Spirit, let us also walk in the Spirit.

5

FRUIT OF THE HOLY SPIRIT

Galatians 5:22-25

But the fruit of the Spirit is love, joy, peace, patience, kindness, goodness, faithfulness, ^{23} gentleness, self-control. Against such there is no law. ^{24} And those who are Christ's have crucified the flesh with its passions and desires. ^{25} If we live in the Spirit, let us also walk in the Spirit.

When we are operating in the gifts of the Holy Spirit and are not motivated by the love of God including the fruit of the Holy Spirit, then the result can be like one that manipulates, controls and is open to divination. People can get off track when they follow a ministry or a vision only, instead of following Jesus Christ and seeking His Kingdom. It is expedient to continue abiding in Christ for the fruit of the Spirit to develop while walking in love. After all, love never fails and to be teachable brings forth everlasting fruit for the glory of God.

Fruit is developed through a process.

- ➢ Forming of the fruit
- ➢ Cultivating during circumstances
- ➢ Activation is up to us

Walking in the Spirit….
Galatians 5:16-18
I say then: Walk in the Spirit, and you shall not fulfill the lust of the flesh. 17 For the flesh lusts against the Spirit, and the Spirit against the flesh; and these are contrary to one another, so that you do not do the things that you wish. 18 But if you are led by the Spirit, you are not under the law.

LOVE
- ➢ Living and Walking in the Fruit of the Holy Spirit
  Galatians 5:22-25
- ➢ Focusing foremost on the first fruit mentioned, which is love and everything flows out of it.
- ➢ God Is Love
  1 John 4:8
- ➢ Perfected in Love
  1 John 4:18 (Agape, unconditional love)
  Love your neighbor as yourself

JOY
There are five different aspects of joy:
- ➢ A new life of joy
  Romans 14:17, Jeremiah 15:16
- ➢ Joy increases
  1 Peter 4:13, John 17:13
- ➢ Joy unspeakable and full of Glory
  1 Peter 1:8, 1 John 1:4, John 17:13
- ➢ Joy without end
  Isaiah 35:10

PEACE
The peace of God surpasses all understanding and comprehension (see Philippians 4:6-7). Jesus Christ is the Prince of Peace and He is encouraging everyone to walk in the peace He has given to us, not the peace the world gives.

The absent of peace will cause us to remain in chaos, but the Lord is showing us a much better way. This is the way of love and when we walk in love, God's peace will always be evident and present. His peace brings a sense of wellness and contentment only received from a place of utter trust and focus on the Lord.

You will keep him in perfect peace, Whose mind is stayed on You, Because he trusts in You. Isaiah 26:3

PATIENCE
The definition of patience is the ability to undergo trials, tribulations and suffering without wavering from our

faithfulness enables us to endure hardship.
Following are some scriptures pertaining to the topic:
Do not become weary in well doing. Galatians 6:9
Patience in trials and temptations. 1 Peter 1:6,7
Patience in discipline and correction. Hebrew 12:11

KINDNESS
Absent of malice
But when the kindness and love of God our Savior appeared, he saved us, not because of righteous things we had done, but because of his mercy. (Titus 3:4-5)

GOODNESS
Uprightness of heart and life
Selfless act on behalf of others

FAITHFULNESS
A faithful person is one with real integrity.
Faithfulness is steadfastness and constancy

GENTLENESS
Also translated "meekness", but does not mean "weakness"
Humility and thankfulness to God
Being polite, restraint behavior towards others

SELF-CONTROL
Self-control ("temperance" in the KJV) is, of course, the ability to control oneself. It involves moderation, constraint, and the ability to say "no" to fleshly temptation.

CHARACTER AND INTEGRITY

A good character is built day by day. Daily decisions build your character. One is tested after a big victory or breakthrough. Therefore, keep your character strong.

We can endeavor to live above reproach , because your good character holds the weight of your vision. JOSEPH is a good example – he never wavered, he had a strong inner character and Joseph impressed God.

Our pursuit should be seeking first the kingdom of God and His righteousness!

When determining the quality of a leader there are excellent guidelines for identifying a God-centered leader.

GOOD CHARACTER – is the sum total of qualities such as integrity, morals and personality. Usually, someone with excellent character, those who allow the Holy Spirit to work in their lives, eventually become great leaders. That usually does not happen overnight. It takes years of testing, preparation and experience.

INTEGRITY – A God-centered leader is full of integrity and highly esteems trust. The leader's yes should be yes and his no should be no. He does not make promises beyond his ability and is dependable. If he says that he is going to do something, he does it!

In Psalm 15 we look at some questions and answers:

Lord who may abide in Your tabernacle? Who may dwell in your Holy Hill?

- Walking uprightly
- Works righteousness
- Speaking truth in the heart
- Does not backbite
- Doesn't do evil to his neighbor
- Doesn't take up a reproach against his friend
- A vile person is despised in his eyes
- Honors those who fear the Lord
- Swears to his own hurt and does not change
- Does not put his money out for usury
- Does not take a bribe against the innocence

He who does these things shall never be moved! The Bible exhorts us to examine yourself whether you are in the faith and to test yourself – *do you not know yourselves, that Jesus Christ is in you? Unless indeed you are disqualified (do not stand the test) 2 Corinthians 13:5*

BIBLICAL DILIGENCE

Becoming a mature leader includes wilderness experiences, which are designed to take us through a process of refining and transforming. During those times we learn what Jesus experienced during His time in the wilderness, being tempted by the devil. He answered every temptation by using the word of God to deter the enemy's schemes. The desert or wilderness seems hot and unbearable, but that is when we learn how to abide in the vine and trust in the Lord with all of our heart.

Soon we detect the streams of refreshing forming in the desert. Those streams in the desert becoming wild, white water rapids and torrents full of God's passionate love igniting, flooding and awakening the dry and thirsty Ones!

Passageways have been forged in our "desert places" teaching us endurance, patience and developing self-control. Those passageways have lead us straight to our Beloved, on Whom we are leaning! A great and mighty harvest is forming out of those times filled with digging deep wells and going deeper in Him.

Psalm 42:7
"Deep calls unto deep at the noise of Your waterfalls; All Your waves and billows have gone over me."

These developments and the spiritual growth into maturity as sons and daughters, will cause us to be a formidable force in times of utter chaos. Empowering us to do all we can in the power of His might and then STAND in and on the promises of our Father.

Soaring higher and yet impacting by going deeper, as we

witness Heaven invading earth and Kingdom manifestations of God's glory to erupt throughout this world.

We can develop biblical diligence becoming persistent, and operate with a pure heart and clean hands, in order for us to see God.

Focusing on and praying about the following scriptures can bring great revelation, building strength and becoming more intimate with the Lord:

Sense of Fulfillment

- ➢ Proverbs 25:12
- ➢ Proverbs 13:4
- ➢ Proverbs 13:11
- ➢ Proverbs 14:23

Bad Patterns

- ➢ Proverbs 21:5
- ➢ Proverbs 12:24
- ➢ Proverbs 13:4
- ➢ Proverbs 18:28
- ➢ Proverbs 13:11
- ➢ Proverbs 14:23

Here are four steps for biblical diligence:

- ➢ Wake up to reality and possible blind-spots.

Proverbs 6:9
- ➢ Define your vision. Proverbs 28:19
- ➢ Effectively partner with others, who are like-minded. Proverbs 15:22
- ➢ Pursue wisdom and build your life on it. Proverbs 16:16

Leadership Qualifications

- ➢ Have a proven ministry (involved in ministry such as Pastoring, Evangelism, Missions, Teaching, Church Administration, Home groups, Worship, the Arts, or Itinerate ministry.
- ➢ Be approved, faithful and accountable to a fellowship of believers

The qualifications for bishops (overseers), as presented in 1 Timothy 3:1-7 and Titus1:5-9, are the norm for all ministers today. In addition, the following groups of attributes are recommended for the ordained minister and leaders in general.

Spiritual Characteristics

- ➢ Love for the Father and Jesus Christ, the ministry, and all people
1 Thessalonians 1:3; 1 Timothy 6:11, 12; 1 John 3:16)
- ➢ Faith (Romans 12:3-8; 2 Corinthians 3:5, 6; 5:18-20;

Ephesians 3:7;4:11; Colossians 1:23-29)
- ➤ Humility (Proverbs 15:33; Romans 12:3)
- ➤ Convictions (Jude 3)
- ➤ Dedication (total commitment to God's will)

Moral Characteristics

- ➤ Integrity (basic honesty and wholeness of character; aspects of integrity are spiritual honesty (Psalm 51:6), intellectual honesty, honesty in preaching, and in everyday dealings)
- ➤ Moral Purity (Isaiah 52:11; Galatians 1:10; 2:11-14; 1 Timothy 6:11-14; 2 Timothy 1:7, 9)

Emotional Characteristics

It is very often that more blunders and failure in the ministry are caused by emotional and personality deficiencies than by ill health, lack of training, education, or talent. Because of this it is most important that the leader be very mature in self-understanding, self-control and healthy emotionally.

The following seven emotional attributes of character are important to the minister:

- ➤ A sanctified temperament (Galatians 5:22, 23)
- ➤ A sense of proportion (balance of humor and seriousness), enthusiasm, realism

- A sense of the beautiful (Philippians 4:8; Titus 1:15)
- Sympathy (Romans 12:15; Hebrews 5:1)
- Patience (Romans 5:1-5; 2 Peter 1:5-8).

Social Traits

- Sociability
- Not Prejudice
- Cooperative Attitude
- Honoring
- Teachable
- Loyalty (to spouse, family, Body of Christ, associates, and friends)

The work of the ministry is both divinely ordered and scripturally set in place in order to establish leadership and equip the Body of Christ to carry out its commission in worshipping God, evangelizing the world, discipling and perfecting the body of Christ.

DAILY IMPACT

Ephesians 5:15-18 Amp
15 Look carefully then how you walk! Live purposefully and worthily and accurately, not as the unwise and witless, but as wise (sensible, intelligent people), 16 Making the very most of the time [buying up each opportunity], because the days are evil. 17

Therefore do not be vague and thoughtless and foolish, but understanding and firmly grasping what the will of the Lord is. 18 And do not get drunk with wine, for that is debauchery; but ever be filled and stimulated with the [Holy] Spirit.

I have quoted and studied above scripture extensively and I like to share the spiritual insight God has given me.

The Lord said He would redeem the time for the days are evil. We are to walk carefully and live purposefully, as wise people and not as foolish ones. How do we walk worthily and accurately? Ephesians 5:17 tells us it is by knowing, understanding and firmly grasping the will of the Father, which will keep us in divine alignment.

I endeavor to manage my time by the leading of the Holy Spirit. If you feel like you have misused your time, take heart, because the Lord can regain what seemed to be lost and give you a fresh start.

My daily decisions, even the minor ones, can over time have a huge impact in my life. My thoughts and intends of my heart affect everything I do and the Lord knows my motives. The motives of the heart must be checked and the developing and maturity of my character is a priority. The Lord is looking for those who are becoming mature sons, whom He can give more authority for a greater impact in their sphere of influence.

To become mature, change is necessary, but contrary to popular belief, change is not difficult in the Spirit. It takes daily consistent small steps, which develop into breakthroughs throughout the year.

> - Learn to change the spiritual atmosphere not just at home, but also wherever you go.
>
> - Ask for godly time management.
>
> - Stop complaining and crumbling, and start by changing your negative thoughts into focusing on things with a good report.
>
> - Tell yourself good news!
>
> - Declare prophetic words over yourself and your family.
>
> - Speak blessings and promises over your spirit daily.
>
> - Do not hang around negative people and stop listening continuously to bad reports.

Look at what God has done in the past and rejoice over the signs, wonders, miracles and answered prayers.

> *JESUS gave gifts to His body, the church, when He ascended into heaven after He showed Himself to His disciples teaching them about the kingdom of God.*
> *(see Acts 1 and Ephesians 4:11)*

6

THE MINISTRY GIFTS-
THE FIVEFOLD MINISTRY

Ephesians 4:11-16 AMP
And [His gifts to the church were varied and] He Himself appointed some as apostles [special messengers, representatives], some as prophets [who speak a new message from God to the people], some as evangelists [who spread the good news of salvation], and some as pastors and teachers [to shepherd and guide and instruct], 12 [and He did this] to fully equip and perfect the saints (God's people) for works of service, to build up the body of Christ [the church]; 13 until we all reach oneness in the faith and in the knowledge of the Son of God, [growing spiritually] to become a mature believer, reaching to the measure of the fullness of Christ [manifesting His spiritual completeness and exercising our spiritual gifts in unity]. 14 So that we are no longer children [spiritually immature], tossed back and forth [like ships on a stormy sea] and carried about by every wind of [shifting] doctrine, by the cunning and trickery of [unscrupulous] men, by the deceitful scheming of people ready to do anything [for personal profit]. 15 But speaking the truth in love [in all

things—both our speech and our lives expressing His truth], let us grow up in all things into Him [following His example] who is the Head—Christ. 16 From Him the whole body [the church, in all its various parts], joined and knitted firmly together by what every joint supplies, when each part is working properly, causes the body to grow and mature, building itself up in [unselfish] love.

Jesus gave gifts to His body, the church, when He ascended into heaven after He showed Himself to His disciples teaching them about the kingdom of God. (see Acts 1)

There are gifts of the Holy Spirit outlined in 1 Corinthians 12 and Motivational gifts in Romans 12, but the gifts referred to here are those outlined in Ephesians 4 and are the Apostles, Prophets, Evangelists, Pastors and Teachers, who are equipping and training the saints to do the work of the ministry. Those are going to be teaching and equipping until all the saints mature, reach an oneness in the faith and in the knowledge of the Son of God. Then we will no longer be like gullible children, but we will be fitly joined and supplying each other what is needed to building each other up in and through God's perfect love.

In this chapter we will get an in depth look into the biblical characteristics of the ministry gifts. We will look at the model of the apostle, prophet, evangelist, pastor and teacher.

These are some of the questions which will be answered:

- ➤ For what purpose did God establish the five-fold ministry?
- ➤ How do I know whether I am called to the five-fold ministry?
- ➤ What price must I pay to be in the five-fold ministry?

According to Ephesians 4:11, Jesus Christ is the God-given Head of the church. It is Jesus, Who GAVE the ministry gifts TO the Body of Christ.

God, the Father, according to 1 Corinthians 12:27-28, CALLS His people into their particular ministry gifts.

A person knows that there is a CALL on his/her life to the Five-fold ministry because there are ALL of the following signs:

A conviction and burning passion in his/her own spirit man, AND a witness and agreement and peace in his/her own spirit man, AND the spiritual equipment (gifts of the Spirit) AND ability to equip and train the Saints.

The fivefold ministry gifts are Apostles, Prophets, Evangelists, Pastors and Teachers.

Effective fivefold ministers not only equip the saints for the work of the ministry, but also help bring the body of Christ to maturity, according to Ephesians 4:11-12. Their purpose and goal as fivefold ministers is to train, equip and prepare believers to be functional in everyday life and to become mature spiritually.

When will the ministry gifts no longer be needed?

When the entire Body of Christ is mature, united in the faith and knowledge of Him, in the full image of Christ and no longer children tossed about by every wind of doctrine blowing their way! The love they have for one another will be evident and they will be jointly fit supplying one to another what is needed.

The gatherings of the Saints will develop organically in and through the unfailing love of God. Victory belongs to them and we will witness the answer to what the Lord said: **"I will build my church and the gates of hell shall not prevail against it."**

The gifts are intended for the advancement of God's kingdom. The fivefold ministers are given great grace and favor to function in their individual roles and callings.

I have learned a very easy and effective way to remember the fivefold gifts and it is by using our four fingers and thumb to represent the fivefold ministry.

Apostle:

The thumb represents the Apostle; it is the one who can touch all of the other four gifts. Apostles set the fellowship/church in order so all the other gifts can function. They establish other saints in their place of ministry.

The Seal or Fruit or Proof of an Apostle is people who are solidly established in the Word and Body of Christ. The Nature of an Apostle is like a Father or Mother (parental) and they Govern.

The four types/classes of Apostles are:
- Jesus the Chief Apostle
- Twelve Apostles of the Lamb (eyewitnesses)
- New Testament/Foundational Apostles
- Today's Apostles who primarily start/found churches

Apostles..
- Keep us founded on Christ
- Some are Wise Master builders; laying foundations for new congregations
- Some apostles are setting things in divine order, in existing churches
- Keeps God's vision before us
- Desire unity and maturity in the body of Christ

Prophet:

The index finger is the prophet. The prophet points in the direction the Lord is speaking to go and they <u>Guide</u>.

"Revelation" gifts are in operation and they are Discerning of spirits, Word of Knowledge, and Word of Wisdom. A New Testament example of a Prophet is Agabus. (Acts 11:28)

Prophet....
- Reveals God's mind and heart to the people
- Reveals vision and opens the revelatory realm
- Activates and stirs up our spiritual gifts
- Encourages us to holy living and righteousness
- Alerts us to seek the manifest presence of Jesus
- Imparts a spirit of prayer, supplication and intercession
- Has a heart to edify, comfort and exhort
- Lays foundations in individuals and ministries upon Christ
- Imparts power and gifts for ministry

Evangelist:

The middle finger is the evangelist, who is out front bringing others to Christ and they <u>Gather</u>. Evangelists get people saved.

Philip is a New Testament example of Evangelist. (see Acts 8) The Evangelist's passion and major message to the world is Salvation in Jesus Christ. The gifts of the Holy Spirit, which are always evident in an Evangelist are Miracles and Gifts of Healing.

Evangelists…
- ➢ Relate to people how to respond to the basic message of salvation, baptism, sanctification, infilling of the Spirit
- ➢ Motivates other believers to share the Gospel
- ➢ Stirs people to move towards God
- ➢ Brings conviction of sins
- ➢ Releases the spirit of repentance
- ➢ Encourages people to receive Christ and become planted in a fellowship within the Body of Christ

Pastor:

The ring finger is the pastor, the one who is married to the Body of Christ/Church and they <u>Guard.</u>

The most well-known and recognized of the fivefold ministry gifts is the Pastor. Jesus Christ is the Great Shepherd of all the church (the sheep) worldwide. The word Pastor means "shepherd". A prominent characteristic of pastors is their love for people and a heart to care for, establish and to see God's people grow and mature. According to the Bible, a pastor is not someone who leads a church and does not fit into the traditional "one-man-show" minister.

Pastors…
- Gathers people in Christ
- Destroys yokes of independence, isolation and insecurity
- Communicates in a way that fosters security and acceptance
- Compassionate and feels with people
- Becomes intimately engaged with the people
- Feeds and leads people and brings them to green pastures

Teacher:

The little finger represents the teacher, who is able to probe into the truths of the Word of God and they <u>Ground.</u> The little finger can be placed into the ear, requiring ears to hear what the Holy Spirit is saying. The teacher has an ability to communicate so that the believers will receive, understand instruction and training by revealing the anointed and living Word of God to them.

According to 1 Corinthians 3, the Body of Christ, His church, is viewed by the Lord as a living and growing garden, which needs to be "watered" by the Word of God. The Word of God is also a light to our path, and to show the way we should go. (see Psalm 119:105, 130 and

Proverbs 6:23).

We acquire faith when we hear the Word of God. (see Romans 10:17). The Word of God heals and delivers. (see Proverbs 4:20-22, Psalms 107:20).

Apollos is an excellent example of a New Testament Teacher. (see Acts 18:24-26)

Teachers…
- Maintain accuracy in handling God's Word
- Deliver people from deception and wrong belief
- Introduce practical application that fits with sound teaching
- Help us to understand God's truth and how to live by principles, not situations and circumstances

****

Remember that here is NO hierarchy or ranking of ministry gifts. No one ministry gift always takes authority or precedence over another. The unity of all of them combined will cause a mighty harmony and impact. When each of the fivefold gifts function and flow together in harmony with the apostolic, assisting to provide oversight and guidance, a mighty force accumulates and it will raise the standard against the enemy. A formidable force will develop against the schemes of the adversary.

It is important to note here, that numerous Marketplace fivefold gifts are placed in businesses on all different levels and influences. We see Marketplace Apostles start businesses and allow the Holy Spirit to lead and guide them resulting in everlasting fruit for His Glory.

7

VISION CASTING

VISION CASTING AND RECEIVING CLEAR PURPOSE AND DIRECTION FROM THE LORD

"Record the vision and inscribe it on tablets, That the one who reads it may run." Habakkuk 2:2

➤ Receiving the vision from the Father
➤ Write the vision and publish it
➤ Praying the vision
➤ Sharing the vision

My prayer is, that God will give you a fresh download of His will and purposes for your life. The vision can be categorized into: time with the Lord, health, marriage, family, ministry and/or business...to name a few.

It is true, that when you receive direction from the

Lord, it can give you clarity and resolve for years to come. With the revelation of the Father's will and purposes comes responsibility. When the Lord shows us, it is so that we can make preparations toward it. We prepare ourselves by seeking His face and remaining in His Presence, by prayer, by soaking and meditating on His Word, by making the necessary surrenders, and by acquiring whatever is needed to fulfill the Father's purposes when the time has come.

In the Old Testament, God's will was determined by the casting of lots, and there was no gamble involved, because of His guided choosing.

> *"The lot is cast into the lap; but the whole disposing thereof is of the Lord."*
> *Proverbs 16:33*

Today we have the precious Holy Spirit, Who is the Spirit of Truth and will lead and guide us into the Father's Truth and will. We can discover how to live and even dwell in the will of the Father and in His Secret Place. Even as Jesus said: ***"My Bread is to do the will of the Father."***

Please take time to seek the Lord for wisdom, knowledge, understanding, direction, and purpose. Consider asking Him such things as the following:

1. What do I sense is God's purpose and vision for me and for the ministry?

2. Where and how will I release this vision?

3. When is the Lord's timing for this vision?

4. How will I prepare?

5. Who do I need to be fitly joined with and what relationships am I assigned to?

6. What are the possible hindrances or obstacles that might prevent me from stepping into this vision?

7. What kind of strategic planning is necessary in order to fulfill this vision?

Ask for divine revelations and strategies from heaven. Secrets and mysteries of God are ready to be released into this generation.

Breaking down the Vision:

Sometime past, I heard someone ask: "How do you eat an entire elephant?" And the answer is: "One bite at a time."

Looking at a vision can be taunting at times, but when we break it down into increments like into goals and then into steps and tasks, it will eventually get all done.

My example will be about writing a book. This was under my category of Ministry. I wrote down what was important in ministry at the time and the first one was writing a book. The steps I needed to take are written down below. After that I assigned tasks to accomplish step by step. It was very evident, that I needed a deadline to be diligent to finish the book soon. During the teaching time we will learn how to break down the vision in a more detailed way.

Examples of Vision for:	**Breaking down into Goals:**
Marriage	Ministry:
Family	Write a book
Health	Missions
Business	Teaching
Ministry	

Steps to Write Books:	**Tasks:**
Research	Jesus time
Self-Publishing	Write daily
Copyrights	Writing exercises
Blogging	Set up

Journaling/Personal Notes

You may want to use a journal to write down all that you perceive God is speaking to you, and reflect on these words. A time of soaking and lingering in His presence can be an added bonus and is pivotal for your intimate walk with the Lord.

A journal is a written record of thoughts, prayers, inspirations, experiences, dreams, observations and revelation. Journaling can be done daily, or only whenever inspired. A leather-bound book, a notebook, a composition booklet or any other means of record keeping can be used to pen down important prompts. It's entirely up to the one journaling.

Bible journaling is a hot topic. There are many wonderful ways to read and study the Bible using journaling techniques. Some can be art and doodling techniques.

- You can highlight and write in the side margins in your handwriting, the way many readers have done it for years.
- You can use the wide-margin Bible and expand your notes to include artistic elements, either stamping, drawing or any other ways you enjoy.

AGREEMENT, ALIGNMENT, ASSIGNMENT

Years ago, I had an encounter with the "Great Cloud of Witnesses" in Heaven. They were standing around a table with four corners discussing what God had planned and what was about to happen on earth. (see Hebrews 12:1) They suddenly turned to me and told me, I needed to be in full agreement with what heaven has planned and the good works the Father has pre-ordained for me to walk out. (see Ephesians 2:10) I agreed and sensed an urgency to do just that.

There is a need to be in full AGREEMENT with the Lord's will and purposes in our lives. Entering into agreement with my heart intentions and receiving internal peace and harmony with my purpose is actually the basis for all assignments to be fulfilled to the fullest.

As soon as we are in agreement, we are placed into ALIGNMENT with God's divine will. Our divine alignment opens us to receive our ASSIGNMENT and we can start walking them out. As we are aligned with God's purposes, we will also be fitly joined with others, with whom we are assigned.

Are you in agreement with the Father's plans? (see Amos 3:3)

> Psalm 42:7
> "Deep calls unto deep at the noise of Your waterfalls; All Your waves and billows have gone over me."

ABOUT THE AUTHOR

Gabriele Gilpin, an ordained minister and graduate of Rhema Bible School, is the President and Founder of Soaring Eagle Ministries, Inc.

During her 25+ years of ministry, she has also served as an apostolic lighthouse leader and overseer, traveling preacher, teacher, conference speaker, translator, missionary and author.

Her vision is international and a part of building the Kingdom of God. The vision includes equipping, training and releasing the saints, to do the work of ministering toward building up Christ's body according to Ephesians 4:12, and to truly "soar on wings as eagles." Many have been transformed by the demonstration of the power of God and His Word.

She has been passionate about developing leadership internationally and has been on television, radio and is hosting an internet radio show. Gabriele has seen numerous salvations, miracles, healings, deliverances, signs and wonders following the preaching of the Word. God's anointing on this ministry has been instrumental in helping many individuals to stir up and release the God-given gifts within them in order to start walking in God's calling and purposes for their lives. The preaching, teaching and prayer ministry releases the fire of the Holy Spirit and a prophetic voice to the hearer.

Gabriele served in Aglow International for nearly 15 years starting in 1991 and was president of Aglow lighthouses in New Jersey, and Florida. She pioneered and started the Aglow lighthouse in Hillsborough, New Jersey, as well as serving on the Northeast Florida Area Team of Aglow International.

Presently, both she and her husband are living in Florida.

For speaking engagements, Rev. Gabriele Gilpin can be contacted by email, phone or the website.

For more information, to partner with us, or to be added to the mailing list, please contact us:

Soaring Eagle Ministries, Inc.
10990 Ft. Caroline Road # 350352,
Jacksonville, FL 32225

Website: www.soaringeagleinc.org
Email: info@soaringeagleinc.org
Follow the Blog: www.soaringeagleinc.org/blog
Like us on the Facebook Page:
https://www.facebook.com/SoaringEagleMinistries

Or listen to Teaching on Internet Radio Talk Shoe
http://www.talkshoe.com/tc/118015

Life Transforming Resources from Soaring Eagle Ministries:

DELIGHT IN THE FATHER OF GLORY:

If interested obtain prices and order online on our website or on Amazon.com:

http://www.amazon.com/Gabriele-Gilpin/e/B00UCBAPLQ
www.soaringeagleinc.org/contactandsupport.html

www.ingramcontent.com/pod-product-compliance
Lightning Source LLC
Chambersburg PA
CBHW061457040426
42450CB00008B/1397